Excerpts From My Soul...
Read Without Prejudice

Nathan Jones

SAJETANIRA PUBLISHING GROUP

P.O. Box 211-0211
Oakland, CA 94604
www.sajetanirapublishing.com

Printed in the USA

Library of Congress Cataloging-in-Publication Data
Jones, Nathan
Excerpts From My Soul...Read Without Prejudice/
Nathan Jones

Edited by Charlotte Y. Williams

ISBN: 978-0-9800747-7-2 (pbk: alk. paper)

Giving thanks to the Creator for His Blessing of another project completed.

This book is dedicated to my family, friends, and to those who have had patience, love, and faith in my dream. You know who you are. God Bless and continue to read!

Table of Contents

5

EXCERPT 1
AFROCENTRIC
ACTUALIZATIONS

An Afrikan Speaks of Home

You are an abyss in my heart, Afrika
My face is full of your blood
These hands God gave me work to come home
I, an Afrikan speaks of the rivers in the Congo
I daydream of the warm summer nights, under
Your heaven

I once sat on a throne, drinking the finest nectars
My kingdom was a dominion of prosperity,
My children played freely in our Garden of Eden
Oh! Afrika, how I long to kiss the soil of your beauty

This continent many called "dark" holds the keys to the
Universe
To life, civilization, and many lands of forgotten nations.
Afrika, my face is full of your blood,
Oh, how I long to return home
To the shores of your warmth and beauty

Afrika, I cannot forget you

10

Elmina - Ghana

shackled in dungeons, quartered by gender   space
limited
caught in matrix prism of darkness
cacophonies sirens the air, dark despair horrific
overseer's eyes watch broken spirits rest on brick beds,
peeking
concrete pillows unwind minds, using excrement *as* linen's
comfort

bodies stacked upon bodies, alive & dead
bodies stacked upon bodies, dead & alive
putrid, the stench, penetrating *my* nasal cavity
my *DNA is* remembering, inhumane traumas altering my
center
resistance! powerless! denigrated! branded! broken! boxed!

alive/   alive/   alive/

stolen from homeland(s), torn from families
centuries later, my center is pushing & unfolding
seared in biblical lamentation, I pray this history never
repeats

||

amazing *Grace*, how horrible the sound, not to save a
wretch?

a wretch i am not?
i am grandma's cayenne pepper
a hot plate of red beans and rice
the sweet savory sweat of sugarcane

Reincarnation

i've ambled through the ages
in shoes well worn
an ancient orphan
many times born
i carry with me
buried deep inside
the memory of an almost forgotten past life.

i hear the waves crash on African shores,
the dust of the *Kalahari* fills my nostrils
all of *Tanzania* and the *Masai* of *Kenya*
i've spied from atop *Kilimanjaro*
i've strolled through the cool jungle
left footsteps along the banks of the *Nile*
the drumbeats of the *Congo*
have played in my head
ever since I was a little child.

i've felt the heavy chains
and separation pains
breathing death's refrains
crushed in the hulls

of stinking slave ships
the salty sweat and sting of whips
descendants of *Ham*, much sinned against
oppression of the spirit
minds driven insane
shackles binding the constricting brain

my belly's been full on grits and black-eyed peas
i've sung in the cotton fields
down on my knees
i've shed crimson blood
cried a flood
and drowned in the *Mississippi*
like *Lady Day*
i'm haunted by black bodies
swaying on "southern trees"
silently screaming the names
lynched ghosts heard by *Billy*

Preamble - Reassembled

We the *colored* People of the United States, in Order to form a more *congruent* Union, establish *fairness*, insure *conjugal* tranquility, provide for the *ordinary* defence, promote the *universal* welfare, and *shelter* the Blessings of Liberty to ourselves and *to All Our Descendants*, do *proclaim* and *institute* this Constitution for the United States of *North* America (Canadians excluded!).

Amendments - *Amended*

* First Amendment – Establishment Clause, Free Exercise Clause; freedom of *any* speech, of *all* press, Freedom of *whatever* Religion, and of *open* assembly; *righteous* petition,

Congress *already made laws respecting* an establishment of religion(s), and prohibited the freedoms exercises; *abridged* the freedom of speech, *corporate pundits plunder the press;* or the right *arms threatened for* people to peaceably assemble, and to *lobby* the Government for a redress of grievances.

Lily In The Valley

if you ain't driving *Mrs. Daisy* or rebelling
In Glory, whose "glory" are you supporting?
a private in the military or being a mammy
In Gone With the Wind... Can't you see just
like the wind you blow like *Lilies in the Valley.*

how many lessons will the *Academy Awards* teach
before we wake up and start our own award show?
is it not enough that *The Piano* grants praise to
a minor, and *What's Love Gotta Do With* gets snubbed.
how could *Bassett and Fishburne* receive no respect?

Othello, a Shakespearean classic no dap, another slap
but *Babe*, a pig gets a nomination
what a slap in the face. I need to inhale over
that *diss*. i am pissed off cause *Quincy* got recognition while
Oprah greeted and served, damn! The *Academy's* got
its' nerve for casting *Mammies, Toms, and Stepin Fetchit*
we are *blackface* cooning the 20th century

Jesse and *Whoopi* provided a cushion of consciousness

in spite of the madness. God did not flex a muscle! once, again
we win in the category of *mu-sick*! great way to pacify
Black folks. Black folks when are you going wake up
and start your own *Academy Award* show?

Black folks in *Hollywood* wake up.
don't you know *Hollow-wood* doesn't
give a hoot about us?

I'm Still Here

Can survival in this onyx shell sustain all the bloodshed,
fears, and tears?
As I recollect on living I think about many of the names
and pejoratives used to describe me. Let me see. I'm been
called: "dumb," "destructive," "dangerous," "deviant,"
"deprived," and "disturbed."
Oh, but it gets better. He's a "drop-out," "delinquent,"
"dope-addict," "street-smart dude," a "welfare pimp," and
"dysfunctional." But I say I'm still here.

Yes Lord, I'm still here.

Even laws have been passed to isolate me from the
mainstream of society.
I've been *Jim Crowed, Grandfather Claused, written down
as 3/5 a person,*
and now Three Strikes and I'm Out. What more can
happen to me
before I cease to exist in this damned Nation?
Alas Babylon, I'm still here. Yes indeed, I'm still here.
Looks like I've failed every attempt to live a life of fruitful
prosperity.

If it were not for frustration, humiliation, and anger I think
life wouldn't be worth
living at all. But I'm still here. Yet I'm perceived as
impulsive, aggressive,
animal-like, and child-like without fail...having natural
rhythm, sensuality,
and uninhibited expressiveness.

Never is my person seen as poetic, creative,
innovative, avant-garde, or assertive.
But by God! I'm still here.
Yes, I'm still here.

The funniest thing about this lifestyle is that I continue to
run into brick walls. Think about it, I'm the last one hired
and the first one fired.
I've been *"black-mailed," "black-listed,"* and *"blackballed."*
And I ask for what? If I had a choice I think I'd rather be
rejected, prejudged, and *discriminated* against. But since I
don't have a choice in the matter,
I'd better thank *Jesus* for all his blessings, right!
Look here. I'm still here.
I'm still around in this chocolate-covered skin.
Yes, I'm still here.

If it wasn't for Grace and Mercy, I'd probably be dead.
Let me tell you, I've been spit on, kicked, shot at,
beat, stabbed, hosed, bit by dogs, even been
hand-cuffed, and thrown in jail.
But look at me, I'm still here.
Yes, that's right, I'm still here.

Man I thought my ancestors had it bad,
but when I add it all up, all of it's bad.
The onyx shell of my fore-parents was chained, beat,
enslaved,
had no human rights, and slave codes were invented to
keep them subdued. And the names were even more
humiliating then the ones I've acquired over the years,
bearing tears and fears.
My ancestors were *"coons," "niggers," "bucks," "*
pickaninnies," "mammies," ""boys," and "uncles."
I never knew that when one grew old one became
white folks' relatives and kin.
But yes, I tell you, I'm still here.
We are still here.
Fascinating ain't it, as to how I can still exist in this
black, bronze, brown, chocolate, pepsi, coco butter, walnut,
chestnut, cafe-au-lait, mocha, auburn, butterscotch,

maroon- orange, maroonish, maures, moorish, sudanic,
ethiopian, onyx, amber, olive, *Mediterranean*, reddish skin,
and still survive the harshest realities, a mound of plights as
high as *Mount Kilimanjaro*,
all in this lifetime and yet be here.

I'm here and I ain't going nowhere.

Out From the Dark We Ascend

Out from the dark we ascend like a lotus plant
we travel throughout history like a joule, a unit of energy
a force like *Newton*'s neutrons moving through a distance
of one
meter in the direction of that force,

We explode in history like an *Atomic* bomb
dispelling the myth of uneducated Africans whose
intellect rivals the talents of *Einstein,* yet surpassing his

In the 21st century we are the hope, the pride, and the
dream
of the formally enslaved *Africans*, 145 years removed from
chattel slavery
and I represent the 5th generation of freedom, a descendant
of a strong willed
african from the shore of the *Canary Islands*, who escaped
the jaws of slavery *two*
years before the *Emancipation Proclamation*

From the degradation of the *Godchaux/Jonas Sugar
Plantation*

to *Bertrainville* to *New Orleans*, to the blessed
Hypolite, Papa, Nolen, Roland, now *me*
the blood of freedom flows through my veins, constantly
we reinvent ourselves like the *Phoenix,* altering our invisible
existence

Running

"I was born by the river in a little tent, and just like the river I've been running ever since"- Sam Cooke

Ran out of my mother's womb
Ran from the slave hunters
Ran from the slave drivers
Ran from the slave castles
Ran from the slave ships
Ran from the missionaries
Ran from shackles
Ran from whips
Ran from dogs
Ran from horses
Ran from guns
Ran from loud sounds
Ran from bounty hunters
Ran from the KKK
Ran from the Military
Ran to the North
Ran to the Hills
Ran to the jungle
Ran from the castles

Ran from pain
Ran from sadness
Ran from stage
Ran to the stage
Ran for the bus
Ran for the train
Ran for the subway
Ran from racial stereotypes
Ran from racial profiling
Ran from being boxed in
Ran from you represent the race
Ran from Niggas and flies
Ran from running
Ran from prejudice
Ran from discrimination
Ran from racism
Ran from responsibility
Ran from hate
Ran to love

Ran from this country
Ran to Canada
Ran to the river to lose the scent
Ran from the Police
Ran from gangs
Ran from gun shots
Ran to work
Ran to school
Ran track
Ran on the football field
Ran on the baseball field
Ran on the basketball court
Ran on the soccer court
Ran the 100 meters, the 200 meters
Ran the 1X100 relays
Ran over hurdles
Ran, representing all nations in the Olympics
My feet are tired of running
Ran from love
Ran from sharecropping
Ran from Reconstruction
Ran from Post-Reconstruction
Ran from Jim Crow
Ran from Segregation

Ran from hurt
Ran from terror
Ran from oppression
Ran from the oppressors
Ran from madness
Seems like I run from everything
Ran from myself
Ran from Jim Crow
Ran from Apartheid

Ran from color only sign

Ran from de jure laws

Ran from de facto laws

Ran from the South

Ran from Code Noir

Ran from Slave Code

Ran from Dislocation

Ran from disenfranchisement

Ran from discrimination

Ran from prejudice

Ran from racism

Ran from mental slavery

Ran from the Projects

Ran from public housing

Ran from the Military

Ran from this country

Ran from the Police

Ran from COINTELPRO

Ran from gangs

Ran from drugs

Ran from the "ghetto"

Ran to work

Ran to school

Ran track

A brotha is always running
"Can't keep running away"- The Pharcyde
Running, running, running
A brother is always running, fast
My feet are tired of running

What Izz Being Black?

What is Black? Is Black synonymous with words wisdom and knowledge? Or knowledge and wisdom? WHAT IS BLACK? And… What is being Black? Definitely NOT a lack of ANYTHING!

I heard someone say that Black is a "state of mind." Well, if Black is a state of mind, you wouldn't mind me giving you a Piece of my mind state as it relates to being Black.

Black is not a color, the last time I checked. I discovered that Black is an ESSENCE, an ESSENCE, an ESSENCE, and yes an ESSENCE that is an efflorescent blessing of CREATIVITY...Not Destruction or NEGATIVITY!

All colors originate from this hue. But what is Black? And what is being Black? Of course there are many Black Carbon Copies perpetrating as Black as BUSA (Black USA would define the term).

You see Black is another whole existence in this Universe; especially in America's chapters and verses.

It appears to me that there is no love giving to Blacks or being Black! But if you're not Black, but act Black, is that equated with being DOWN or COOL? Is Black a "state of mind" or a game changing sign of the time?

"into the sixties
a word was born........Black
& with black came poets
& from the poet's ball point came:
black doubleblack purpleblack blue black beenblack was
black daybefore yesterday blackerthan ultrablack super
black blackblack yellowblack nigger black black whi-teman
blackerthanyoueverbes 1/4 black unblack coldblack clear
black my momma's blackererthanyourmomma
pimpleblack fall
black so black we can't even see you black on black in
black by black technically black mantanblack winter
black coolblack 360degreesblack coalblack midnight
black black when it's convenient rustyblack moonblack
black starblack summerblack electronblack spaceman
black shoeshineblack jimshoeblack underwearblack ugly
black auntjemimablack, uncleben'sriceblack williebest
black blackis beautiful I justdiscoveredblack negro
black unsubstanceblack." --Haki Madhubuti

and Black become synonymous with A Movement in the 70s
and James Brown echoed a voice for all Blacks ---"Say IT Loud I'm Black and I'm Proud!"
Ungawa Black Power...
Black Love
Black on Black Crime
Black Orpheus
Black Church
Black Psychology
Black Studies
Black Leaders
Black House
Black Schools
Black Education
Black Muslim
Black People
Black Music
Black Noise
Black Vote
Black Community
Black Economics
and the Black Bourgeoisie
Black First...the 1st Black

Black Mayor

Black Caucus

Black Graduations

Black House

Black Nation/ Black Nationhood

Black Joy Black Tears

and Last the Black Experience!!!!

So what is being Black? What is Black?

Is Black a cultural manifestation of my (utamaroho)?

behaviors

attitudes

values

ideas

language

symbols

rituals

inventions

mores

traditions

ceremonies

customs

beliefs and practices

31

and what is the Cultural (template or Aspects) of being Black? (utamawazo)
What is the black ethos?
What is the Black world view?
What is the Black Ideology?

and what is the black cultural (core) factors ?
(asili):germ/seed of a cultural essence.
What is the Ontology (nature of being; Essence?), what is the Cosmology (origin/structure of Universe?), what is the Axiology (primary/Character of universal relations?) of being black!!!

When I think of being black I think of a Nation that exists within a Nation as Essence that
manifests and revels itself to all...

Some might still argue that Black is a 'state of mind'--it is more like a "state of emergency"...

You see Black is synonymous with land (Nubia, Akebulan, Sudan, and Ethiopia) meaning land of the burnt face people. Now that's Black!

Black is synonymous with Creativity's Past, Present, and
Future.

Black is fashion:
Fubu
Phat Farm, Baby Phat Farm
Willi Wear (let's not forget the original trendsetters!!)
Johnny Blaze
Karl Kani
Wu Tang Wear
to name a few…

Black is Musical Innovation, Avant-Garde,
conceptionalization of musical inspiration
Black is Negro Spirituals
Black is Gospel (You know as in God's Spell)
Black is Jazz,
Black is Creole Songs,
Black is Rock & Roll, Old soul
Black is Rhythm and Blues
Black is Funk
Black is Big Band, Swing
Black is Bebop

Black is Miles, Flying High

Black is Rap

Black is Neo-Soul

Black is House

Black is Screw--DJ Screw

Black is Dirty South Bounce Sound

Black is Heavy Metal-Purple Haze Baby!

Black is Charlie Parker nurturing Miles

Black is Thelonious nurturing Coltrane-A Real Love
Supreme

Black is cool like Lester Young

Black is Blue Notes (trying to find the notes in between
notes)

Black is Motown-Smokey, The Temptations, The
Supremes, Stevie, and Lionel

Black is Stax, Motown

Black is Sax ways, the way Coltrane plays

Black is rhythm

Black is Atlantic

Black is Otis, Percy, Cooke, and Donnie Hathaway singing
Young, Gifted and Black is Minnie

Black is Marian Anderson and Leontyne Price

Black is Ella, Billie (Lady Day), Bessie Smith, and Etta James

Black is Def Jam, Uptown,

What is Black? What is being Black?

Is being black equated with Ghetto, or is it a state of being?

I guess being black is American Popular Culture...It's cool to be Ghetto Fabulous!

But before we use the terms let's understand the mindset and the origin!!!!

Black is Dance artistry, Black is movement articulation:

Black is/was Alvin Ailey, Judith Jamison

Black is Fatimah, Debbie Allen,

Black is Breaking, Poppying, House, Capoeira,

What is being Black? Is it now cultural appropriation?

The "cool pose," the strut in one's walk

Is it the way your clothes hang and sag?

Is it the speak bravado one chooses to use?

Is it the way one breaks verbs?

Black is Intellect:

Black is Padmore

Black is Cornel West

Black is Henry Louis Gates

Black is Michael Eric Dyson

Black is Derrick Bell

Black is Molefi Asante

Black is Ivan Van Sertima

Black is John Henry Clarke

Black is John Hope Franklin

Black is Oba T'Shaka

Black is Wade Nobles

Black is Cheik Anta Diop

Black is Booker T Washington

Black is W.E.B. DuBois

Black is Martin Delany

Black is Marcus Garvey

Black is Padmore

Black is CRL James

Black is JA Rogers

Black is Rodney

Black is St. Clark Drake

Black is Walter Rodney

Black is George James

Black is Amiri Baraka

Black is Anthony Bowder

Black is Asa Hilliard

Black is Naim Akbar

Black is Malcolm X

Black is Martin Luther King

Black is Carter G. Woodson

Black is A Leon Higginbotham Jr.
Black is Spike Lee
Black is Langston Hughes

Being Black is social conditioning, upbringing, and way of life!
Being Black is universal community connections!
If you get stop by the PoPo for driving a new car, then you Black
If you get followed by undercover cops in shopping malls, then you are black
If assumption about your abilities come into question about academic achievement
I suggest you Watch Finding Forrester!!!--Black is Potential
If by chance you are from the inner city and you are a black male over 6ft. 200lbs, you must play ball!
If you are between the ages 14-25, in jail, on drugs, or dead, you must be black or an endangered species.

Black is Rage
Black is Essence
Black is Consciousness
Black is a Lotus Plant
Black is not Limpbizkit, Eminem, or Bubba Sparks

What is being Black? Ask me, I'll tell you.

I am Black!

Condensory

African descent
Preferential treatment
in airports.

Privilege associated with interrogation
No apparent reason,
Because content of one's skin.

The elites' hospitality
Reserved for the guilty
Who trod a *just* path.

Hazel Scott

Long before Alicia Keys there was…there was Hazel
Hazel Scott, a protégé of Billie Holiday

Sixty-one years (1920- 1981)
Your extraordinary talent graced our lobes

Caribbean born: Port-au-Prince, Trinidad and Tobago
A pianist and musical child prodigy

Juilliard trained, before Juilliard *trained at age 8*
Playing *Carnegie Hall* was not a dream, but a conquest

Five motion pictures: *Something To Shout About,*
I Dood It, Broadway Rhythm,
The Heat's On, and
Rhapsody in Blue.

Classical, Jazz, Blues, Boogie-Woogie, and ballads,
she played the piano with a grace and effort unparalleled to
any other

She could take you from Bach to Boogie, fusing Classical
music with Jazz
They called this style swinging the Classics, playing
Romanoff straight

Adding base notes, syncopating the rhythms and turning
classical arrangements into Swing

The first Black woman to have her own show: "The Hazel
Scott Show"
DuMont Network aired her program from 3 July to 29
September 1950

She earned hundreds of thousands of dollars in her time
Didn't allow discrimination to keep her from earning her
just due

She stood up & spoke truth to power, when Black Artists
were banned
From performing in Constitutional Hall in Washington
DC, she kicked the door open

$5,000 a show, she wouldn't perform in front of segregated
audiences

If she was requested to do so, there was a no-show!

Still she got paid…that was in the Contract…
Two months on the air, opposition to McCarthyism &
racial segregation, cancellation

A *Communist* in question, something Paul *Robeson* could
relate to?
Scandalized your name, ill-humanity often brings joy and
pain

Charles Mingus and Max Roach, a debut album *Relaxed
Piano Moods*
On a Debut Record label matched with success, Hazel Scott
always put to the test

Once scandalized because of her affair and a subsequent
marriage to Harlem's Congressman,
Adam Clayton Powell Jr., she played the background but
never lost music ground

Her Black star power popularity predated Barack and
Michelle Obama

Hazel and Clayton were the toast of Harlem and its Blues,
blues

Lost in obscurity in the States, but *Paris*: The City of Light
opened a warm embrace
Nina Simone and Sidney Bechet could understand her pain,
no Blackballs or Blacklist
A warmed embrace for a musical A-List

Hazel, you were before Alicia and always will be.
History knows. I hope Karen Chilton tells your story with
integrity

African in America

Being an African in America
one cannot help but feel
his dual identity.

His dichotomous nature is
what sustains his very presence
existence and essence in a land
that recognizes him not.

Distant Beat

I am not a simile, metaphor, or a fading symbol.
This you hear is not a breeze softly blowing a tree.
I am not a black strip of asphalt being trampled over.
It is I who express emotions of laughter, pain, and joy.

I cry rivers because I exist, here on Earth,
My voice sings like a choir moving a congregation,
These are the designs of my humanity, my voice.
I speak them, and my hands write them.

I am a poet with a depth of ancestral lines.
Lines connecting me back to an African beginning.

Is it my soul you hear drumming against your heart?
Or am I just a phantom lurking in the dark?
I am not a fading symbol, simile, or metaphor.

Black (Man's) Beauty

Once called a wood-chucker, a monkey, and a savage brute in his homeland, Africa, thousands of miles across the *Trans-Atlantic,* his color and character are further diminished. He is called a *brute, a coon, a natural athlete, a spook, a darkie, a jigaboo, and a nigger.* Names given simply to denigrate and inflict internalized hatred of himself. But what of the pure and unadulterated essence, what of the "well" that holds the key to all the world's hues? What of the beauty of the black man?

Known as masons of the world, *architects, scientists, artists, inventors, explorers, pedagogues, mathematicians,* and the sages of ancient and modern *African* wisdom. What of the beauty of a Black man? How can myths and stereotypes be so powerful that they permeate the heart and soul of our "essence"? One cried out, claiming he was invisible to a culture that refused to recognize his presence. One man had a dream that all would be able to unite in racial harmony. One man spoke on the ills society projects on its native sons. One man cried, by any means necessary. One man echoed, up, up yea mighty race, and accomplish what you will.

One man shouted, I'm Black and I'm proud. And another coined the phrase "black is beautiful." But, I ask, what of the beauty of a black man? Shall we really keep hope alive? The beauty of a black man, the strain on this amazing creation is nothing less than remarkable. Many nights he's cried and sang the ebony blues, yet his soul is not defused.

Did you see that bronze paragon soar through the air? Did you see that ebony powerhouse cover that field in 9.5 seconds flat? Did you hear that riff in his vocal cords? Have you read the literature of *Langston, Wright, Dunbar, Mosley, McKay, Bontemps?* What of the beauty of a black man? I read somewhere that a black man was responsible for the first *open heart surgery.* I read somewhere that a black man was ingenious for the *transplant of plasma.* I read somewhere that a brother was responsible for the first surgical *separation of Siamese twins.*

Did you know Banneker, a black man, designed the Capital of the US? And I have my suspicions about the *Cotton Gin* and its inventors. Did you know a black man was responsible for the creation of the cell phone, the golf tee, typewriter, elevator, fountain pen and traffic signal?

What about the beauty of the black man? I heard somewhere that he is wise, spiritual, intelligent, honest, loveable, and loyal, a great family man, a husband, a father, a friend, a lover, a confidant, and a sage.

Did you know that much of your music was created by a Count, a Duke, a King, and the Ambassador? Boy how stressful can the beauty of a black man be? His mentality is oppositional, yet he operates under pressure with his "cool pose" displaying his integrity and openness. What of the beauty of a black man?

I heard my sistas say the black man's beauty lies in his ebony sensuous skin. Some sistas echo the beauty is in his baldhead, that shines like a flame in a dark palace. I heard many sistas suggest the beauty lies in his dreadlocks. Can she run her fingers through your dreads? Yes, you can! I saw many sistas quiver and shiver at the bass in the voice of Barry. But what is it about the beauty of a black man? The beauty is dynamic, regal, pleasant and diversified.

Maybe the beauty exists in his strut, his laid back way of talking, or his jazzy and flarish personality? He's definitely got the ownership on "cool" and he's definitely nobody's fool. But what is the beauty of the black man?

The beauty lies in his essence, his culture, his food, his dance, his song, his color, his presence, his speech, his walk, his intellect, and the universe of his being. A spirit that many emulate but can never replicate, the beauty of a black man.

The Smell of Racism

The putrid stench of racism paralyzes my soul like a carcass deteriorating in the heat of the dessert relentlessly being taunted by a vulture. Hell has no fury like the scorn of *Racism*. It smells so trite, so vilifying, so malevolent; never tolerant always on the move, *racism*.

The rancid odor permeates the so-called finest of institutions, seeping through the crevices of solid foundations tainted with many colors of "blood" oozing from pained and imprisoned souls, lurking to break the shackles and fetters of a pernicious nemesis seldom opposed. Yet, the smell of racism overwhelms *"America the Beautiful."*

Racism and its stench manifests its dysfunctional and fearless antics in-and-out of the fabrics of this nation leaving all crippled, hurt, and disillusioned feeling the sting of its vicious attacks. The smell of racism, remember the aroma of the abyss of the well that holds all the keys to the ills of this world. *Race-ism*, oh! How sweet the smell?

Nigga, You Still Around?

Shackled, enslaved, beat down and blood oozing from my
Crown.
All this pain and shame is enough to bring my spirit down.
When I look up to see my *King's* throne I see a brighter
heaven
than I've never known.

After Massa beat me he said, "Nigga you still around
lappin' your blood
bleeding from your head?" I paused before I spoke. And I
said, "White man
is this a joke? You might beat me, you might break a bone
or two, but I tell you
what before this day is through, the resilience and buoyancy
in my might will cause you damnation, *massa* when I
fight."

You may ask, "Nigga are you still around." But come in my
time I'll still be around to take back many stolen crowns.
Nigga, you still around?
Nigga, you are still around?

Oh yeah, White man, I am still here and I know you fear my brown. And if you look, you'll find I exist throughout many Amerikkkan towns, being the Nigga stealing your "crowns."

But you ask me Nigga, you still around?

Why I Vote?

__The Civil Rights Act of 1866__ is a piece of United States legislation that gave further rights to the freed slaves after the end of the American Civil War

This was an Act created to counter the Black Codes of the rural South

__Black Codes__ were laws passed on the state and local level mainly in the rural Southern states in the United States to limit the civil rights and civil liberties of African Americans.

It was the domination of the Republicans in the-United States Congress passed the act in March 1866, as a counterattack against the Black Codes in the southern United States, which had been recently enacted by all former slave states following the passage of the Thirteenth Amendment to the United States Constitution.

…and in his ignorance, President Andrew Johnson vetoed the bill, saying Africans were not qualified for

United States citizenship and that the bill would "operate in favor of the colored and against the white race

- ✓ Civil Rights Act of 1866, extending the rights of emancipated slaves.
- ✓ Civil Rights Act of 1871, also known as the Ku Klux Klan Act.
- ✓ Civil Rights Act of 1875, prohibiting discrimination in "public accommodations," found unconstitutional in 1883.
- ✓ Civil Rights Act of 1957, establishing the Civil Rights Commission.
- ✓ Civil Rights Act of 1960, establishing federal inspection of local voter registration polls.
- ✓ Civil Rights Act of 1964, prohibiting discrimination based on race, color, religion, sex, and national origin by federal and state governments as well as some public places.
- ✓ Civil Rights Act of 1968, also known as the Fair Housing Act
- ✓ Civil Rights Act of 1991, regulating discrimination claims.

The Mississippi Plan of 1875 was devised by the Democratic Party to overthrow the Republican Party by organized violence, suppression of the black vote and disruption of elections, in order to regain political control of the legislature and governor's office. The Mississippi Plan was also adopted by white Democrats in South Carolina and Louisiana.

A **poll tax, head tax, or capitation** is a tax of a uniform, fixed amount per individual (as opposed to a percentage of income). When a corvée is commuted for cash payment, in effect it becomes a poll tax (and vice versa, if a poll tax obligation can be worked off). Such taxes were important sources of revenue for many governments from ancient times until the 19th century, but not since. There have been several famous (and infamous) cases of poll taxes in history, notably a tax formerly required for voting in parts of the United States that was often designed to disenfranchise poor people, including African Americans, Native Americans, and white people of non-British descent.

Literacy Test refers to the government practice of testing the literacy of potential citizens at the federal level, and potential voters at the state level. The federal government first employed literacy tests as part of the immigration process in 1917. Southern state legislatures employed literacy tests as part of the voter registration process as early as the late nineteenth century.

Grand Father Clause: The original grandfather clauses were contained in new state constitutions and Jim Crow laws passed from 1890 to 1910 in much of the Southern United States to prevent blacks, Native Americans, Mexican Americans, and certain whites from voting.[1] Earlier prohibitions on voting in place prior to 1870 were nullified by the Fifteenth Amendment. In response, some states passed laws requiring poll taxes or supposed literacy tests from would-be voters. An exemption to these requirements was made for all persons allowed to vote before the American Civil War, and any of their descendants. The term was born from the fact that the law tied the then-current generation's voting rights to those of their grandfathers. According to Black's Law Dictionary, some southern states adopted constitutional provisions exempting from the literacy requirements descendants of those who fought in the army or navy of the United States or of the Confederate States during a time of war.

Jim Crow Laws were state and local laws enacted between 1876 and 1965. They mandated de jure segregation in all public facilities, with a "separate but equal" status for black Americans and members of other non-white racial grousps.

Filibuster, or "talking out a bill", is a form of obstruction in a legislature or other decision-making body. An attempt is made to infinitely extend debate upon a proposal in order to delay the progress or completely prevent a vote on the proposal taking place.

Dred Scott - *Dred Scott v. Sandford,* 60 U.S. (19 How.) 393 (1857), was a decision by the United States Supreme Court that ruled that people of African descent imported into the United States and held as slaves, or their descendants[2]—whether or not they were slaves—could never be citizens of the United States, and that the United States Congress had no authority to prohibit slavery in federal territories. The Court also ruled that slaves could not sue in court, and that slaves—as chattel or private property—could not be taken away from their owners without due process.

De Jure Laws - in Classical Latin *de iure*) means "of law", as contrasted with ***de facto***, which means "in fact".

De Facto Laws - is a Latin expression that means "of the fact" or "in practice" but not ordained by law.

The terms *de jure and de facto* are used instead of "in principle" and "in practice", respectively, when one is describing political or legal situations.

In a legal context, *de jure* is also translated as "by law". A practice may exist *de facto*, where for example the people obey a contract as though there were a law enforcing it yet there is no such law. A process known as "desuetude" may allow *de facto* practices to replace obsolete laws. On the other hand, practices may exist *de jure* and not be obeyed or observed by the people.

Plessy v. Ferguson, 163 U.S. 537 (1896), is a landmark United States Supreme Court decision in the jurisprudence of the United States, upholding the constitutionality of racial segregation even in public accommodations (particularly railroads), under the doctrine of "separate but equal".

Too many people fought and died for my freedom, for my freedom to vote

It was 1968 when my mother was able to vote. She was 22 years old

My grand-mother, my mother's mom, didn't vote until her early 50s

My mother's grand-father couldn't vote because of *Jim Crow! The Grand-Father Clause! KKK Terrorism! Intimidation!*

My mother's great-grand-uncle couldn't vote (*died at age 108*) when my mother was 13 years old

My mother's great-great-grand-father couldn't vote

…and today, I am watching history take place.

I thank *Shirley Chisholm*

I thank *Jesse Jackson*

You pioneered our progress

Why do I vote?

Why do I vote?

WHY DO I VOTE?

I vote because I have always known this right, this freedom.

Uhuru Sasa!!!!!

The Day After A Black Man Became President

5th November 2008, a day after the most historic moment in America, a day realized, actualized, and manifested. For the first time in US history on Election Day, a Black Man, a Black Man, not just any Black man, but a global, world-citizen, family oriented, hyper-intelligent, cool, calm, and down-to-earth brother made HISTORY. Some call it the "Joshua Era,"40 years after the death of Martin Luther King Jr., I call it a "long time coming."

The second coming is here, and the spirit of history has guided and allowed Barack Obama to take center stage of American history and the world. Yesterday was a victory for every African brought here to this land: shamed, shackled, tarred, fettered, abused mentally, physically, socially, psychologically, torn culturally, and spiritually beaten down. This was the hope and dream of the enslaved. This was a piece of Dr. Martin Luther King Jr. dream being realized, and all those indefatigable freedom fighters pushing for change and equality in Babylon. I know Jon Hypolite, Paul Jones, Nolan Jones, Roland Jones, and all my ancestors from my father's lineage are rejoicing and rolling over in their gravesites, talking, laughing, eating, drinking, stomping, shouting, and dancing in Congo Square to a "small" day of victory and redemption.

This is for the 8 generations of Carsons and Grays on my mother's side of the family. I wonder what the revolutionaries and freedom fighters such as Nat Turner, Gabriel Prosser, Denmark Vesey, Harriet Tubman, Frederick Douglass, Sojourner Truth, Booker T. Washington, W.E.B. Du Bois, Langston Hughes, Paul Robeson, Martin Delany, Alain Locke, James Baldwin, Malcolm X (El- Hajj Malik El-Shabazz), and Ozzie Davis would say? Wow! A Black Man, a Black Woman, and their beautiful brown, auburn, amber, cocoa, chocolate, walnut, mocha, cappuccino colored skinned daughters, all being Black in the White House. The Obamas are the first to be the First Black Family in the White House! We have come a long ways since the hauls of the slave ships, to the slave house, to building the White House, and now we living in the White House. Barack, Michelle, and their children will be at the head of the dinner table, and not as servants or Civil Rights invited guests.

Will Jeremiah Wright be invited? Will Jesse Jackson be invited? Will Berry Gordy be there with Motown? Will the spirit of Fela Kute be there? Will Maya Angelou be there? Will Coltrane's and Miles' Jazz be there? Will Mandela and Bishop Tutu be there? Will World Music fill the air? Will we hear Africans drumming, djembe, batas, congas, etc? I can see, smile, taste, touch, and hear the celebrating. The earth is rejoicing.

What will be the culinary delights for their first dinner? Red beans and rice, gumbo, fried chicken, collard greens, corn bread, potato salad, green pies, and black-eye peas (good tidings for the New Year), candy yams, pecan pie, bread pudding, who knows? I can picture Afro-sheen, pomade, Frankincense and myrrh, Shea butter in the bathroom cabinets, flat irons, and pressing combs.

You know there will be barbershop talk, hair salon talk, south-side Chicago politics being discussed.

Will the walls and hallways be adorned with African kings, queens, and dignitaries?

Some echoed, "Rosa sat so Martin could walk, Martin walked so Obama could run. Obama is running so our children can fly". Jay-Z said, "What more can I say?"

I say, No More Grandfather Clauses, No More Poll Taxes, No More Mississippi Plans, and No More Literacy Tests, No More Paramilitary attacks, Red Shirts, Rifle Clubs, and No More KKK intimidation tactics.

Will the image of the Black men in America finally change? Will those looking inside realize there is more to us as Black men than just playing sports, being rappers, musicians, and sexual objectified objects?

Will our young finally believe they can be anything they dream, and have whatever they desire?

These were my thoughts on the day a Black man became President of the United States.

EXCERPT II
ROOTS AND BRANCHES

Coda: Black Man Who Are You?

You have come a long ways since the *Trans-Atlantic*
Triangle Slave Trade
Stolen from sacred ground
Tarred, fettered, and humiliated
Walked for days, no rest, no sleep
Taken to Slave River
Bathed: the Last Stand erupts
Canons used to overcome a *Pyrrhic* victory

Next Process...

Held in slave dungeons
No light. Only darkness
No solitude, but loneliness
Tongues silenced
Slave ship: 30, 60, 90 days
Horrific journeys
Can you imagine?

Next Lifetime...

Wall Street
Auctioned off
Sold and bought
Forced to labor on *Plantations*
No Freedom
Insurrection! Uprising! Resistance!

Maroon societies
Underground Railroads
North Star
Freedom Up North
Philly, Nova Scotia
Europe?
Today…Now

Black President

Son of the South

I am a son of the South
The grandchild of the *Grandfather Clause*, the literate of the
literacy test
I am the tower towering over the *poll taxes*
My mother was *Ruby Bridges*, and my grandmother *Rosa
Parks*,
a feisty little lady of Afro-Cherokee descent.
I sauntered the land of creoles, quadroons, octoroons, and
PFWs
Jefferson invented this formula of how my Black is defined,
numerically
I bathe in the *Bayou*, I inhale *Big Easy* smells, and I rode the
waterways of the *swamps, I am a full-grown alligator*
I wrestled with gators and used water moccasins *cotton
mouths* for lassos
The *Neville Brothers* beat Bayou sounds into my body,
Irma Thomas serenaded my soul with Voodoo blues
I devour *Popeye's Chicken* and ravish *Poor Boy* sandwiches
I snacked on *Choupiqu*e (shoe-pick), with *Louisiana Hot
Sauce* (tastes like chicken)
Bourbon Street dazzles me with its plantation decadence

I caravan *Canal Street* looking for *Lake Pontchartrain*
I vigil hollow tomb gravesites
I tap danced on sea-shelled paved roads absorbing pox of
water under my sole
Thanksgiving swings with the *Bayou Classic* (100,000)
adorned chocolate people
The celebration is political
I am decked out in ostrich plume and beaded designs of
Black Indian Mardi Gras attire
Politicians and gangsters pay for their progeny at *Tulane.*
Congo Square beats the ghostly sounds of *gourds, banzas, &*
bamboulas
honoring formerly enslaved Africans.
We dance freely to unforgotten beats and rhythms of home

Born/Change/Transformation

I.

<u>Born</u>

Breathe, push, breathe, push
Breathe, push, breathe, push
You are almost, there!!!

"It's a baby boy," proclaims the doctor
Her second baby boy, the dream continues

Mama cries, mama's happy, mama's sad
Are those tears of joy or pain?
Why is mama crying?

II.

<u>Place/Time/Med. - Decision</u>

Public hospital, *Charity*
Thursday, 8:10 pm: Born (*Yaw*)

Circumcision! Hard decision! Her decision!
An awkward position, whose commission?
Dad complains of Mama, admission.

Living in *Voodoo* land is strange
People have wise tales,
Tales are often true?

III.

<u>Birth Certificate</u>

What is your race?
What is your color?
The Certificate reads: "Negro"

What did my father's Birth Certificate read?
Did it read, Colored, Negro or what?
What did Papa's *BC* read?
I can't imagine what Hypolite's certificate read!

Gun Shot

Mama and baby fall to the floor.
Tears overcome *mama's* eyes
She yells back in defense.

*"YOU WILL NEVER PUT YOUR HANDS ON ME
AGAIN!"*

The floor creaks. Footsteps quickly calculate.
Screech the closet door.

Click… Click…

BOOM!

Is all I heard at 3 p.m. when mama shot dad in his right leg.

New Orleans Living: The Beginning

I am grandma's cayenne pepper in a hot plate of red beans
and rice
We children are the sweet sweat of sugarcane lingering
from her lips
Her progeny satiates a parched mouth and spirit.

Working from can't see to can't see,
blood-sweat drips into 6 generations
DNA connects bloodlines like jigsaw puzzles bringing me
forth.

My muscle memory conjures long laborious days in the hot
sun
I need Ruby's bucket of blood and a voodoo dance to calm
my pain
New Orleans is gumbo Congo west, isolated
We conjure the ocean ancestors to take us higher.

His Image

64 years ago my father was born
7 years and 2 months ago he died
They say I look like my father
They say I am boisterous like my father
They say my mannerism is like *Yogi* (my father)
They say certain facial expressions are his likeness
A relative during in 2003 a family reunion commented:
"Looks like *Yogi*, walks like *Yogi*, sounds like Yogi
Must be *Yogi*"

Are we reincarnations of physical images?

My dad I am not.
Never wanted to be like him
After I heard the Gun shot…

Experiential Education

In New Orleans we were *Black*
I come from the South
Haiti's sister city the *Grandfather Clause State*
The land of quadroons (1/4) and octoroons (1/8)
The land where the Spanish 1/16 rule of Black blood qualifies
Your racial and social identity
Congo Square: Africa is remembered/ Angola Prison: souls are captive
The French Quarter, Patois, and Creole Talk
Chopique fish cooking in propane
Sugarcane and a machete symbolize "never again."
Bayou Talking… (*for true, don't play wit-me no*)
The Second Line, rejoicing no more physical suffering
This was southern comfort Blackness
There was no question of your identity?
Black was/is/will be, and going to always be Black
Unless you had a touch of Choctaw or Blackfoot in the Mix!
Geography splits the mind like the *Mason Dixon Line*
I live in the west, the home of Prop. 21, 187, and 209
In California, where we are everything, but *Black*

Our education is different and identity is experimental
But we identified as we, sometime everything but Black.

Black Pride

Whatever happened to Black Pride?
Did you go on vacation? Have you gone to hide?
Or did you just die?
Do you remember when Black pride was so high,
So high like those circular crazy hairstyles
That drove people wild
Upon sight of African might.
Remember when brothers and sisters were poets,
You know the Black Poets
Or was it the Last Poets;
The words that trickled off their lips were
As smooth as a cool bottle of Moet.
Black pride have you gone to hide?
Remember Angelou-- "Phenomenal Woman" or
"Still I Rise..."

Was that not the epitome of Black Pride?
What about the pulsating words of Brown—
"I'm Black and I'm Proud!" Dare we not say it LOUD!
Black pride have you gotten lost in a crowd,
Where your radiant hue cannot howl?

Remember when brothers and sisters were getting "high"
on knowledge
and getting strung out on "love"?
Remember when black was beautiful?
Remember when brothers packed knowledge
And not gats?
Remember when Black love was as pure
As a raven from the heavens above!
Remember when musicians were musicians and
Not studio artists?
Remember when EWF--(The Elements) sung about
"Devotion"?
Remember when the nigga died and
Black folks were let in?
Remember when the nigga died and
Black folks were let in?
Black Pride, I thought I caught wind of you the other day.
Black pride I thought I saw your face on T.V.
I thought I heard your voice on the radio.
Black Pride do you remember Stokely, Newton, and
Rap Brown?
How resilient, how resonating were the sounds.
Black Pride, did you give up your pride

For a suit and a tie?

Inside My Skin

i am a reincarnation of *Roland, his* progeny.
my *DNA's* mannerisms imprint his likeness.
i am *born* the second of four siblings, the first middle a son?
i emerged from mama's womb wailing *Bayou blues,*
making a splash before *Jimi* played *Woodstock.*

born, big, boisterous, bold, brave, and bodaciously *Black*
before entering a room my spirit swallows the atmosphere
my color shows up before I do, causing reactions…?
i'd like to think of myself as visibly, invisible.

Would *Ellison* approve?

i can't *blend,* i can't *hide,* and I won't *apologize*
for my intimidating size! Do others?
my stature is menacing to some, maybe?
and people make all kinds of as-sump-tions.

i am stereotyped as virulent, strong, and a *Superman*?
should weakness illustrate, *then* I am wimp?
when I err, my humanity is questioned?

when I err, my humanity is questioned?
can't be human, because Black doesn't = humanity
is there a safe place for me to my mind without reprisal?
tip-toeing and tap dancing was *Stepin' Fetchit*
at least *Lincoln Theodore Monroe Andrew Perry* made his
millions
his two minds had two phone lines, *Stepin (Hollywood) and
Lincoln (Chicago Defender)*
From Superman to Man, JA Rogers, I comprehend.

my voice is truncated to save face...
in the corporate world, i am asked to shirk my personality
speak with softness, be humble, be cognizant of
communication, always *smile*.
hands are in my pocket or behind me, standing with my
feet together with *precision*.
"tap dance around the truth," they say. but, truth severs
employment.
i shift from relaxed to authentically *Black* man pose.
there's no place for my spirit to relax, as my emotions are
consistently taxed.

stress +mental enslavement is a recipe for death

i was born by a river… and like the river i have been
running ever since…
and…my soul has grown weary like *Langston's* rivers
i question, when can my skin get some rest?

a ritual is met...

my silent rage is serenaded by controversial hip-hop
anthems like
Fight The Power (PE) and *Fuck the Police (NWA)*
syncopated with rhythmic bass shootin' my subconcious
leaving holes bustin' at the seams...screams! screams!
i watch my 3rd eye vision fade
blood cascade over hazy stained unstable foundations
while verse and prose are the only wars I win hands down
i shadow box with *Newton's* law of gravity staying afloat
running! dodging! hiding! and bouncing between checks -
check it!
I'm emasculated and castrated by *Amerikkka's* white picket
fences
in my night and day mares
potatoes and rice sashay across my mind
my daughter comprehends my ends with –"ok daddy!"
my ritual is met with pit-stops to *Mickey Ds and B King*
(unhealthy sting operations)
savoring the morsel of a processed chicken meal and fries
we step over the homeless, signs in hand "I'll work for
food."

coins drop in a paper cups, watching hopeless dreams being
fulfilled, momentarily
Prayer House Apostolic Church throws out a raft for
salvation
but my *Mothership* was floating upon eclectic trips
righteous words and scripture couldn't save me
nor harmonious chants and voices laced with spiritual
strings or bass
that curdle my blood stream
i embrace my daughter for dear life
praying that a Marvel character would liberate her
from the *Deluge* of life's pressures
i close my eyes tight and wish upon *North Star*
because many a lotus grew
and originated
from the black of my mind

Pushin' A Pen...And Receiving No Dividends

feeling tired like *Spenser for Hire*.
a brotha's soul and mind is burning like *Hell's Kitchen* fire.
my body is metamorphosing into an amorphous
dimension, feeling the pinch of a meager pension,
contemplation... dissension... perhaps an
uprising fore-mentioned
as my energies seek retirement from psychological
detention,
my pockets are frozen deep in a subtle form of
matriarchal financial suspension.

where the brothas at? we need male energy
and balance to create a win-win.
finding hope to save our *Black* children,
but finding no means to
employ or implement hope to save the *Poor Righteous
Teacher*. yeah, we be teaching, but the hierarchy is sucking
our blood like leeches.

hope seems dim, working under modified servility, being paid slave wages,
turning academic pages, hoping to create a *new* generation of sages...
but where's the love for *Generation X* as it ages?

praises come in multiple forms.
"he's an asset" a colleague annotates.
"he's a blessing to the *Academy*" one remarks.
Praises are all I get as the shit gets
thick like the *fat lady* who sings. but it's not over.
I feel like I entered *The 36 Chambers* of the *Wu Tang*,
Not knowing when the illusion will manifest into reality.
but my reality is a philosophical fallacy,
breached in an *Afrikan-centered* principality.
yet i'm *pushing a "pen"* while my talents are being prayed upon like a hen in a lion's den.
constantly preaching to *Man Child in a Promised Land*, my mission is to pull disillusioned Afrikan children from a gutter of disparity,
but my efforts become *undermined and neutralized*
by pseudo-righteous charities...Still the *Poor Righteous Teacher* speaks and

sees with clarity. Lost in a community attempting to
rewrite our history, deconstructing and reconstructing the
misgivings of afflictions, lies stacked like
Mounds of the ancients in Mississippi still chased
by the "ghost" of masta's hounds. but we, me, he, the
Poor Righteous Teacher is asked to "stick around."
my reflection in the mirror appears to be a back-lash from
the *Pre-Civil Rights Movement* and *the Black Movement*
intertwined into one...
still looking down the face of the barrel of a gun.
feelin' like I'm *Public Enemy Number One.*
i'm subdued mentally, economically, and financially.
this profession is not glamorous, sheik nor substantial.
i'm running through dark shafts with fetters on my feet.
this shit is so bleak, i'm forced to take my message to the
streets.
surviving the struggle is cliché and old,
it's time for me to break the mold.
sell me a new line of hope, not a line of white dope.
that shit is for the fiends...but you think i'm bein' mean?
i think it's time for you to come clean.

Pushin' A Pen...And Receiving No Dividends.....

Looking Out The Window

I moved from Jack London's paradise to Kaiser's industrial
wasteland.
When the blinds come up and I look through my window, I
see Ham's children
Walking the streets of shattered hopes and broken dreams,
Like Langston's *A Dream Deferred.*
I understand that my reality is *The Matrix*--I took the
conscious pill.

The universe where I exist is not lavish or adorned like a
Hollywood Disney Movie. When the rubber from my tires
kisses the asphalt and travels *Down Harbor Way*, it tells a
uniquely different kind of story; something strikingly
familiar, reminiscent of Spike's *A Tale From The Hood.* If
dreams were not deferred, perhaps some of my stories
could relate to a *Beverly Hills 90210*, and not a modern day
Rosewood or *Black Wall Street* tale: the kind of tales that ills
a comatose spirit.

As much angst as I experience from day-to-day,

I still find myself feeling like Ellison's *Invisible Man,* yet the paradox, it would seem, is that I attract more attention than Wright's *Native Son*: Bigger Thomas.

Why in 1999, and I'm not dreaming as I write this...when I look out the window, I see not a *Henry Louis Gates Jr.* Nor a *Cornel West Breaking Bread* about *Race Matters?* Instead, my eyes are privy to recent historical tragedies. Brothas being shot, prostitutes selling God's gift to humanity (insanity), a liquor store on every block, a *Barber Shop*, a church in a 3-block radius of another church and a funeral home to complement the death that took place the night before. *Dead Presidents* seem to thrive from the lethal misfortunes of would-be beautiful *Black potentials.*

My parents don't boast about the good old days of the '60s. It's not nostalgic like Yuppies listening to *Motown* hits like *Glenn Close and William Hurt* in *The Big Chill.* In fact, they don't have time to chill, nor stop to get caught up in the moment of passivity: cause when the action and *The Movement* end,

We lose sight when we look outside that *Window.*

Mattie Rich's *Inkwell* shed the best light on a possible *Big Chill,* but

when one checks the content and recognizes the
dysfunctionality of the *Black* family, chills abound.
Aberrant forms of acculturation in its purest form
Perpetuates Afro-centric castration.
Where's the holiness in that?..
Some might ask, how does it feel to be in the *"Land of Milk
and Honey"*?
My response is, "soullessness."
As I move from illusion to disillusion, where a bridge
separates me from the wealth of this nation, I still think of
the white kids at the college on top of a hill.
Although *Affirmative my Actions* might be
No one really gives a damn, about me.

Let Go…

You are dismissed
Go home

Your services
No longer needed

There are no benefits
Find another team

You missed an opportunity
Our practices are standard

Relationships are important
Consider his/her team

Your services
No longer needed

Memory of Impression

An almost forgotten past life, *Baobob* roots
Many times born, I carry with me buried deep inside
The sobriety of societal loss

I was once a child raised by the earth, wind, and fire
My voice spoke the language of the ancients,
Kemetic, kinetic, cosmic: dialects of divinity

The drumbeats of the djembe, djun, and the bata
Have played in my head ever since I was a child
Learning communication through sacred codes, unspoken
My memory is long, fragmented and tormented

I have sung in the cane field, laughed and cried in the
cotton fields
Down on my knees, I have shed crimson blood, cried a
monsoon
Drowned in the Mississippi and the Chattanooga, too
I'm haunted by Black bodies swaying
Swaying on "southern trees", strange fruit
Lynched, without sanctuary, silently screaming

Billie sung it
I cannot forget
I cannot forget
My DNA tells this story often
It's in the blood memory of my muscles
My memory is seared like a hot iron

Pains of heavy chains, I felt nooses around my neck
Separation pains of severed genitals and body parts,
displayed
Breathing in death's refrain
Crushed in the hulls of sinking slave ships
Cried from the salty stings of whips
Rats, roaches, and unknown creatures brushes my skin
The shame remains embedded, hidden in ancestral veins

To Mourn A Ritual

Apnea kills my nights
Sleeplessness introduces insomnia
Rest lacks, creating longer days.

Outside my window cats sound sirens in heat.
Skunk stenches perfume the air, alarming nasal cavities
Raccoons rummage, ravishing protected waste.

Sensibilities stretch lunar oblivion, despondent.

My mind evanesces, transcending spatial boundaries.

It's 6:00 am again and I am consciously-unconsciously
awakened

KPFA blares, filling my room with broadcast sounds
Democracy Now! boasts another *Amy Goodman's* bulletin
Sound-boarding domestically global politics
Eardrum dances. This is *Democracy Now!*
Getting up is optional, I lay there 15 minutes

S S S…

Ritual! Routine! Repetition!

Off to the Plantation…

A Poet Unknown

A poet unknown alone on the *Streets,*
Lost and humble as a strayed *Sheep,*
Somebody well read, articulate, profoundly *deep.*
An unknown poet that's *me.*

An unknown poet in despair, undiscovered
With 'poetry' *much* to share, desiring
Praise for works complete, no publishing
Deal cannot deplete.

Prolifically I write as Langston,
I'm articulate as gracefully as Dunbar,
I speak as passionately as Angelou.
Who knows? Will I be *decomposed* before it shows?

Discovered, please not too late I hope,
But I drudge through and I continue to cope.
Dreams of being known this is true
But if no-one reads me: will I be through?

An unknown poet is what I *be,*

Whether rich, famed, or undiscovered you see
the only thing I could ever dream to be is a
Talented poet hey that's *me*.

De-Constructing Masculinity

A typical near-synonym of masculinity is virility (from Latin vir, man); and the usual complement is femininity

If I deconstructed my masculinity what kind of man would I be? Who would I be if I deconstructed, the concept of masculinity or its antithesis femininity?
A sistah asked me to call her Daddy, so in return I asked her to call me Mama. When I asked her why, she replied, "I am in control." During the rules of engagement I was a bit confused, but not lost. So, I played along.

The woman is guilty of the masculinity myth.
It is masculine to open the door for a lady?
To put one's coat over a puddle
To stand when a woman sits at the table
To protect his family
To provide for his family
To support his family
To do all those things his mother requires of him
Mother's love their boys and raise their daughters…

How can I deconstruct what mother (the woman) has built and created?

I got my game from my mama

Got my name from my mama

Learned how to fight from my mama

Learned how to talk to lady from mama

Learned how to treat a lady from my mama

Mama even taught me how to tie my necktie.

Shine my shoes, clean a house, and cook my food

The feminine taught me my history

The feminine gave me:

My skin

My culture

My race

My name

My identity

My nature

My essence

My language

My manhood

The fundamental essence of my asili

Brothas Be...

brothas be battling Babylon while
bomb shelling poison to da babies,
maybe they helped create lives at stake,
pushing and peddling drugs,
cuz thug is the mentality,
living pseudo-life styles, a dead man's reality
pimping a surrealistic paganistic devilish trip,
just to sip the "Amerikkkan Dream"
love Amerikkkan style enough to drive a "brotha" wild.
dead and gone like a stillborn child.
mama didn't raise murderers, pushers, and pimps to
span a generation of empty vessels,
hollow like a *Columbus* voyage.
dead Souls spreading death to young chocolate souls,
hot like coal, fuckin' up many positive would-be molds
silly ass simps, don't know that slavery is mental,
like an imp that pimps you to take negative actions on
your own Black seeds, not knowing
you choppin' down lives like acres of weed
sold and smoked, as you choke, taking a toke to make
your scrill screwing, the pill, she chills,

a baby born, and Babylon exalts the ills.

Tuskegee, Aids, Ebola…

brothas don't be knowin'

conspiracy is white supremacy.

I mean the point is to change the joint.

the joint of fast cars, fast women,

fast cash, fast ass, and fast lives

that don't make the night or dawn because

a mentality and respect for life is gone.

but brothas be knowin'

that the caged bird sings, behind bars, helping to create

more laws while the freed is scarred, soft and not hard, but

pressed.

oppressed, depressed, suppressed, and hard-pressed to

escape

babylon's chores

brotha's need to be knowin' that the end is near.

slavery is mental and there's much to fear.

It's past time, we need to change our minds

can't afford strange fruit

dangling from the vines of

estranged Black Thought. The price is too high

for Black Souls sold and bought.

How can heaven forgive us
If we slit our own throats?
If deadly conspiracies
dictate our reality
the inevitability is   our people's fatality.

How I Kick Linguistics in the Game

1996 Streets of Urban Communities (street)

Yo! What's up patna? I heard you gonna be at the crib
parlaying withcha ya girl.
Yeah, Nigga I'm gonna be at the spot chillin' with tha
Misses.
Nigga, before you be on Lock-down let's kick it for a
minute and make some scrill
At tha spot. You down Nigga. Yeah, I'm down but let me
hit this BOMB and gin
So I can get my "perv" on. Alight.... Alight! Man, did you
see them Bitches perpetrating
In that Benz. Yeah fool, they was all that.

At the Work Place 1996 (customary)

Hey! How are you brotha? Man I'm maintaining. How's life
treating you. Ah, It's o.k. I'm just
Hoping I can get this managerial position at the job. I've
worked too hard not be considered

For this position. I knowledgeable of the job, I have great costumer relations, excellent
Computer skills, etc. Mr. Johnson have you sent in my Letter of Recommendation to the Entry
Level Management Training Program. Yes, I did but they've all ready made their selections
For this next class. Sir, Why don't I get accepted into the program. Son, you are very intelligent,
Educated, and smart. But I think your attitude needs to change in terms of how you treat our
Customers. I think that if you do this, I see no reason why you don't get promoted. O.k. Mr. Johnson.
Thanks, for that advise. Mutha Fucker how many excuses will be made before I get my promotion.

At the College/University 1995 (cultural exchange)

Saalem alakum my brothers. Alakum-saalem brother. Are you a Muslim? Nah! I really don't
Buy into some of the militant philosphies and idealogies. Come on granted they have some good
Things and some bad things to offer. But no, Islam is not for me....Professor do you need any help

On this coming quarter's Research Team. I think that your theories of Black men and Black women
were well researched and appropriate. Oh yeah. Have you completed my Letter of Recommendation
for NYU. Yes, I did soon you can pick up your copy from the Sociology Department. It's waiting at my Secretary's desk.

At Kimball's East 1995 (formal-informal)

Good evening my beautiful Nubian sistas. You look very gorgeous in your black satin dress. Thank you brother Asete. Are you ready for a night filled with romance and ambiance? Yes I am. You know Will Downing is one of my favorite vocalist, and Luther has nothing on this talented brotha. Baby, you know you are right...(I feel you on that). So, do you have a significant other? No! I'm just dating and testing the waters. Likewise. Perhaps we can do lunch during the week? Yes, that would be such a wonderful inducement.

Frantz Fanon stated, "Mastery of language affords remarkable power." I guess duality in language is not a fool's reality. This is how I kick my linguistics in the game.

The Hot Shit

Can we talk about some hot new shit?
Like dismantling racial profiling shit
Because, I am tired of the same ole psychological bull shit.
Do we have a new slogan or pitch to confront?
The same old American political dead shit
I want to hear some new shit about what you discovered
shit.
I want to hear about your new song, your new dance, your
new life
Your new job, your new house, your new love, your new
history your
New baby shit
Can we just get along shit? Smoke some trees and see
beyond this shit?
Now that we have some new hot shit! A new shit, that's
fresh like a morning "shit"!
Can we catch a fire from this new shit?
A new-age fiery nice shit, the righteous shit. That keeps you
moving shit!
Are you tired of the same old storied shit?
We all talk about the same old shit.

Shit unlike the shit we talked about last night, last week, month or last year.

Are you ready for the next shit? I am tired of being constipated, and it's time to let go of the old shit.

A Promise

13 years ago I vowed a promise

> Still no charm bracelet

In Egypt, I bought you an 18karat gold *scarab* and a
Cartouche
…to be continued…when I saw you several months later,
Christmas,

> you conveyed a heartbreaker: "Dad, I am
> allergic to gold"

My happiness was crushed,
the pain of my vertebra snapping under an elephant's foot

Again, no motherly communication, shots in the dark of a
healthy child

13-4, and 9 of them I was in tune. A foreigner I am,
looking into the window
of your life. Strange, isn't it?

> *Distance is a bitch!!!*

EXCERPT III
TRUTH DISCLOSED

Revolutionary Erotica

My phallic point spills wetness all over this page
Every drop takes a new direction in pointillism, artistic
surrealism
Each drop creates a different sensation,
Touch, taste, smell, sight, sounds ticking the senses
Like honey from my scepter
We are the Tantra of past/present times
Revolution is the way we create love, eternally
Inhibitions rendered freely
Liberation sexing outside the box of normality
Bodies of silhouetted images
Human clay, Earth!
God's first Adam and Eve, spiritually human, not divine
Exiting sheltered warmth from isolation,
Stimulation, galvanization, tantalization
Stepping into cosmic paradise, rolling their carnal dice
Naked, baptized by heaven's tears
I sculpt you with lyrical clay
You manifest, acquiesce, and evanesce
Time becomes ancient recollections
I cannot decipher romantic Sanskrit, but I understand my
personal love script

Love's revelations, mysterious taboos, world's unknown,
indifference
Straddling the fences between Afro/Euro sensibility
Duality, duplicity, dichotomy, multiplicities
Complicity of complexities, invisible destinies
Patience is patience
And my nature is complex, perplexed, compelling, next,
next, next...
Traveling cultural odysseys
Reflection of a soul's rebirth, terse
What is my worth? What is my value? I am a metaphoric
Black Stallion
Loving the sexual drug, the high, the bliss-never dismissed
Experimentation, other colored skins, I'm in, questions
abound
Objectifications, fallacies twisted, like political jargon
Accepted taboos of aberrant bullshit! (BS)-unwarranted
tests, I flex
Black noise screams from my lips of
Sax ways, jazz ways, ways ahead, dazed...Aged!
Turning musical pages, invoking ancestral sages
Hearing verses of divine speech, vintage
Perfect like Christ's spiritual cipher, non-decipherable

Sacrificing one discipline, for prophesy sake, my inner-
poise quake
A soul lost to non-spiritual temptation,
One less predestination, sometimes stress in celestial
destination
Revolutionary erotica, the erotic is revolutionary
Tales from the catacombs, underground
Surviving on hollow ground
The dead live on throughout the pages of history
I catch spirits in the wind, like Native Dream catchers
While souls excavated
Exploited like Hottentots backside
Euro sexual African treasured prizes
Colored pussies suffer from neo-colonial rape
Forced sterilization and experimental surgery, vilifying!
Xenophobic pirates decimate my pre-existence
Don't be ashamed of the shamed,
For the same shame causes inter-generational pains
Racists' myths perpetuate ignorant energies
Cultivating dilution, convolution, and pollution
Tarnished and tainted, wearing Fanon's mask
Depth of one's essence is lost like "progressive theory"
And politically incorrect rhetoric
I stand at the juxtapositions of life/death/rebirth

Spiritual intimacy confuses my mind
Like verses from Songs of Solomon
Challenging traditions of sacred psychosexual,
metaphysical
And spiritual inter-connectedness, apprehension is my life's
"raft"
Traditional rituals become caricatures, distortions of my
existence
And now my psyche vacillates as a pendulum   between
Afro-Euro synthesis
An American antithesis
A symbiosis, a mirage of life
Levels of capitalistic conditioning and bargaining
Hope is chronic bliss
Life's corruptions, interruptions
An asili suppressed by Euro odysseys
Like a junkie's hopeless vision of reality
Nigods are vanquished
Straddling cultural identity
Caught up in the plight of others
Sex, love, taboos…
Angelic manifestations rescues my soul
I dance because it is my "Messiah," my liberation

Living between erotic fantasies, lost in a prism of carnal and sacred
Desires to integrate other worlds
Acceptance never achieved, an anomaly always perceived
Experimentations become my soundtrack of lived interludes
Black metaphors keep me dancing in the tenses of time
Diverse women from times past, was it love or a fad?
Fading...
Memory of memoirs rarely understood, I understand, over-stood
Encryptions intimacies are scripted on the papyrus of my soul's chest
Passion is lost in a silhouette of kaleidoscopes
Multiple African relationships cultural mixing
Amalgamations (new races/faces) miscegenation once [outlawed]
And hope manifest its complexities in profound moments of anxieties
Provocative lessons in Black and White... strife...we fight!
For an education in necro (death)
Mirroring the reflection of consciousness
/unconsciousness?
Rebirth, a new renaissance in humanity

Cultural pride is exemplified
Sold   Bought
             Packaged
                     Repackaged
                             Pressed
    Distributed
             Manufactured
                     Marketed
                             Advertised
Managed and
             Produced
We buy! We sell! We buy! We sell! …
And live the lie of perpetuated hells
Cultural integrity is questioned?
Identity is manipulated through
Cultural theft is confusing, misusing and distorting our
minds
Minds are not sound because race and sex hounds the flesh
It massages the mind like a 1960's psychedelic drug
Jimi understood the trip, *Purple Haze*, baby
Music, dance and rhythm cures the curse
Music, dance, and rhythm cures the curse
Music, dance, and rhythm cures the curse
Of Babylon yet the beast lives on

The revolution is erotic, erotic, erotic, erotic…

Shining

I am light shining on a peacefully fierce chutzpah
I am lunar interludes, starry nights, and moon kisses

Earth is my solace and ground my foundation
Can I exit in dual realities, a twin-ness of existence?

Will I transcend this lifetime?
A life that pastures a litany of illusions

Of mother, of father, of earth
I speak with twin-ness of tongue, deciphering multiple
worlds
I am not tongue-doubled, yet I speak in coded languages

Am I contrived of the many pains of my ancestry?
I am visibly invisible to many, but not to sum
I force and compel others to feel my presence
My voice is lethally shy, but resonates with passion

At night I dream of life, and at day of death
My future is unknown, so I exist in three tenses: present,
past, and future

I have no time for the "now" it's all an illusion
Of mother, of father, which equals birth
Of water, of earth, which equals life
Whose life?
This is a prelude to my dream...
I am now awake.

A Moment in the Port...

she impregnated me with the swell of her words
causing a chemical reaction, compelling me not resist
the devilish divine in her eyes while incited
a special brew of tears, charming me like a vampire
conjuring *Phoenix* tears to ease my weariness of her
(*Voodoo* love potion)
she arranged special tears to acquire my undivided
attention
her countenance was enticing, her deep bluesy eyes, wild,
untamed, precarious like a white water rapid, discretely
pursued my spirit, i could see the animalistic pheromones
lifting of her skin like steam discernible from a body after a
hot shower. like *Medusa* they mesmerized

momentarily my mortality became subdued and petrified
but presumed mortification from this vixen caused a
moment of serendipity
the meaning of my life's vision was interrupted as a
frequency change on a *Sirius Satellite Dish:* in that
moment's encounter, everything i thought ceased to make
sense

she filled with me fantasies impossibilities
but heaven isn't supposed to be on earth?
maybe it is and i just haven't realized it, yet?
this moment was a threshold of precipitation, a dangerous
one.
she was enticement, with the subtle sting of a *Black* widow;
her charm was poisonous but not too deadly where I
couldn't get an immediate antidote.

her eyes communicated sartorial splendor
she looked at me with heart shaped-teardrops streaming
down either side of her face
she was water adapting to every situation, creeping,
flowing, crashing with force, and forming to the content of
her environment.
i was the content of her environment.
i knew this woman was a "paragon in passing" what to do?
how was i to counter the voodoo she possessed?

she stared at me as if I had written *Aristotle's 1000* books, or
as if i was a *Mount Everest, the Tour Eiffel,* or the
Conquering Lion of Judah.
i was not the norm in her eyes, but a secretive prized
treasured,

a surreptitious she would come to despise, once she's
subjugated her mission
what of her motives, i wondered? her motivations intrigued
me! i was praying not to enter the *Dutchman's* lair
was it my position in life? was it the letters behind my
name, my Ph.d?
was it my professorship? was it the way I dressed, or how I
captivated her with the way I articulated and broke my
verbs?
i am guessing i was symbolic of the *La Concorde or the*
Washington Monument, two *phallic* replicas heisted from
East African shores
i wasn't a pauper, but a prince in her mind's eye because of
education tides
i was strange and forbidden fruit on all accounts, but the
Queen's rhetoric was my saving grace, although i spoke
with a peculiar ethno-centrism and an *Akebulan* hipster
swagger.

we shared isolated elegance in privileged communities
co-existing in the pit of academic and educational valor,
the decadence of old money and trained snobbery, was the
connect

she sensed this, again while trapping me with hearts shaped tears,

tears as acidic as a *Komodo Dragon's* bite

she had an agenda, an objective, and a power point.

if i play, would i pay? what are the stakes?

we vanished into the night, a radiate skyline

oak trees, city lights, misty air, refreshed by *August* rain

we communicated outside the collegiate arena

her perfumed aura was reminiscent of a *New England Aristocrat*

we ended up at *The Rustic*; an old monkish gothic restaurant,

lights dimmed, candle lit tables, yuppies all encompassing, stares

before i realized, i was indulging the wonders of the five *Ws (world, weed, wine, word, and woman)*.

next...her flat, secured intimacy, sweet poison, with no chances of death

she plays obscure *Blue Note Jazz* tunes on an antique *Olson and Bang*

we end up in time like a *Duke Ellington* composition, suspending our disbelief as we graft a surreal interlude; we pass the time with *Basie, King-Cole, and Vaughn*

her love was like a *Bordeaux, Cabernet-Merlot, Pinot and Syrah* wine, mixtures
red, passionate, varying textures, warm, wet and sensuous;
i watched the claws of her wine stream down the glass of my body.
we made *African and European* pillow noises
serenading each other with unspoken communication.
we loved like a well-researched college dissertation
using critical elements to dissect our intersections.
prologues, acknowledgments, introductions, abstracts
footnoting, end-noting, MLA references, citations, indexes
annotated bibliographies, and commentaries fostered
scientific reasoning.

her presentation was phenomenally exceptional
she was trained to be detail oriented
she followed her passions, as she traveled down the *Nile* in awe of the wonders
of *African* mythology searching for *Solomon Mine*,
her eyes focused on my sepia landscape, soiled from geyser interludes
she was trained to be detail oriented, as she meticulously observed the rising and setting of the son,
she swooned the warmth of *Earth's* centripetal forces

127

although polar difference existed, *Pangaea* resurfaced
leaving *Continental Drift* to biological interfacing.

she passed all her oral exams efficaciously with honors
in the end, she questioned, "does academic achievement
entitles you to relinquish your *African* upbringing?"
her question hit harder than a *New York* minute.
all i could remember was a woman standing in front of
telling me, suggesting, we have something in common…
a "sartorial splendor" of sorts.
i recognized in that instant, i will always be invisible to
sum…and that the truth is best served silent.

Life Is A Series of Sound Bytes

A series of snapshots into the mind of an artist
You have to write the script, the words, and create the
screenplay of your life
Take one step at a time
Find your words
Remember the events in your life
Write about them
Put voice to words,
Put characters to events,
Place scenarios into perspective
Remember
Past events can never be relived or duplicated
Every moment is an adventure!
So cherish the moments of your life!
This is not Groundhog Day, the movie, a repetition of
events
Allow your words, your life, and your experience to serve as
a miracle for others
Remember those special encounters, the unforgettable
moments
The memories that continuously bring a smile to your spirit

Remember your first bike lesson, and how you fell on your face, and how you still Managed to conquer Mt. Everest.

Remember your first day in school

Your first love

Your first kiss,

Your first date

Your first dance

Your first heartbreak, and how the world just came to an end!

Your first day in Middle/High School!

Prom Night

Your first real job

Your first paycheck

The first hour of learning a new system at work

Your first day of college

Your first crush on a teacher

Remember life is a series of snapshots and sound bytes!

Remember

Enjoy those surreal pulp-fiction, unthinkable life altering moments

If your life is one fish bowl of banality, write about it!

If your life is a comedy, a history, or a tragedy, write about it!

Everyone can't be a Shakespeare, a Hemingway, a
Steinbeck, a Baldwin, or Wright
But you do have a right to capture your life on paper, film,
video, CD, record, tape, or whatever recording device
pleases you.
If Sundance or IFC picks up your life, then you have more
snapshots and sound bytes
Just don't subject your creative genius to the likes of
Hilton-We all don't want to visit Paris!
Remember
Capture your childhood, your adolescence, and your rites-
of-passage into adulthood
Don't forget the path that you've journeyed to get you
there/here
Every moment in life is like spinning a wheel of fortune-
you win some, you lose some
Promote yourself
Manage yourself
Be your own booking agent
Market yourself
Publish and distribute yourself
Make your life count!
Be the actor in your own movie, for only you can play you
the best

Dictate what you do best! Exercise it, perform it, and sell it to the highest bidder

Make sure your investment in self reap you residual income.

Remember, life is a series of sound bytes.

Darkness

I arise from a depth filled slumber, tainted
with
unwarranted mares stifling my ease,
comatose I remain slippin' into a
peculiar darkness. Searching for a tangible
solace…   reaching…
into Black Hole images
amorphous

Shapeless & eccentric like minds of
creatures

roaming Earth's pastures
Unseen by my 3rd eye vision
I'm dizzy from academic
missions

from…wishin' and fishin'…turnin'
pages and
seekin' sages…
my soul burns
explanations I yearn

133

blood pressure rises and falls
like Bay Area weather
my search
empty
as I lie comatose
slippin' in
Black Hole
spaces....amorphous.

134

The Souls of the Streets

Dreaming
I ascend from horrific odysseys
Traveling in time and space
Unconsciously moving throughout history
On human road maps, sketched in sap,

drip,

down,

open

spines

Hearing voices in my sleep, feeling legions of
Souls calling out, strange fruit hanging from trees without
sanctuary
No proper burials and tears of loved ones crying rivers of
pain
Pain with roots as deep as a Baobob tree
I rest my breath on the wings of my ancestors
Acknowledging their strength while exuding an
unrelenting will to manifest me,   their future.
The souls of the streets are calling
The souls of the streets are calling
The streets of the souls are calling
The streets of the souls are calling

135

I hear them and cannot ignore their cries
Their spirits are seeking, trying to find a way
　　　…Home…
their spirits are intricate bloodlines
impressions pressed upon paved dirt roads
fossilized like prehistoric plants
telling stories unknown, memories chained, unchained
the souls of the streets are pushing through concrete
In vacant lots trying to find,
　　　...Home…
but home is not home anymore
the land is soiled, unfamiliar and foreign
their pains are experienced through the soles of my feet
the blood from the sacrificed fertilizes the back roads of
humanity
the blood from the sacrificed fertilizes the road backs of
humanity
struggling and fighting to reconnect to family trees that
have been
cut off from Afrikan histories
here I stand in the dawn of pre-existence juxtaposing two
worlds,
indifference
dreaming, walking the back roads of

places unfamiliar trying to find that Crossroad where
an ancestor made a deal with the devil
Billy sung it, and Nina tongued it.
That lead me to this hell
The souls of the streets are calling
The souls of the streets are calling
The streets of the souls are calling
The streets of the souls are calling
And I am catching the hell they felt
through bloodlines of hope.
I need my Dream-catcher
I feel them, they see me, but I don't see them as I descend
from
Horrific odysseys trying to find home again
Scattered throughout time and space like atoms
Not wanting to be that amoeba that attracts
But when I awake, I realize I am those very souls
That are calling, and looking for a road map
Conjuring ...home...

Walking

Walking around my home suspicious
Looking outside cornered windows

Watching

Crack being sucked up by my family
Vampires sucking the blood from
Unsuspecting innocent victims, bystanders

The dawn sets in
Chants are faintly echoed in wind
Holistic chants and prayers, syncopate in Baptist rhythms
The *Holy Ghost* is trapped in the sanctity of the sanctuary
And God's unchanging hands don't rescue the wretched

God's oasis is right across the black asphalt
Where are the spiritual warriors, while war is waging in the
streets?

Voices are loud and faint, creating nightly musical rhythms
Caricatures distorted cacophonies distress my sleep
patterns

138

Prostitutes stroll *Webster* thinking salient strolls go
unnoticed
But son (Sun) misses nothing-questions ensue?
Playing in the backyard lost in his world of plastic action
figures

Innocent and not affected by the world outside of his world
He's protected by high canopy fences and bushes
Camouflaging his peaceful oasis

Strangely, unfamiliar, bodies of pale content hibernate in
Old money owned structures
The man's neo- hipster children have returned back to the
block,
Babylon, now, a haven for his prodigal sons and daughters
of yester-year
Gentrification smells the streets…a twisted odor of
unwanted pre-destiny
Evergreen Church is greener with new *Jericho Walls* built to
God's
Third Heaven

Suspiciously walking in my room,
Looking outside cornered windows,

Expecting change in paradise
But change is gentrified housing
Laid back living for those who have come back to reclaim
A land deemed undesirable.

Time To Chill; Enjoy Life

The world is dying, the world is dying and no-one seem to have an answer
Or a cure, for a rapidly deteriorating community.

Everything is moving faster
Than a microwave produced dinner.

The world is dying and I am wondering what we as a people will do
To prevent mass death and destruction.

It is time to come together for the preservation of all humanity.
How do we clean up the mess that has been made?

Wrath of a Woman

The words she spoke were as powerful as the Great Deluge.
Passionate, wanting, honest and sincere, they were
I tried to elude this flood of words,
I kept drowning and sinking to the bottom of the ocean
floor.
The more she spoke, the more repudiated, rebuked, and
chastised, I was.
Woe is me!
Woe is me!
What can I do?
When will my head surface above this water, this water of
death?
Her Deluge is nature's destruction.
Help me to survive.
I need a desert of dry thought!

Language Change

Language change
Linguistic strains
Mental chains
Communication tamed
Re-defined over time
New verbiage
Our tongues entwine
Like southern vines
Around Germanic
Romantic discourse
Enslavement has forced
Inventive dialects
Neither Mother's nor Father's tongue
Shades and shadows
Memories lost
Yet we understand in codes
Created by a will to survive
Pains from separation's trauma
Rites of passages
Lives taken during the *Middle Passage*
Voices of European savages
Pigeon tongues, tongues shackled

Dual identities form   *dichotomies*

Human survival is the norm

Dichotomies circumvent,

We constantly invent

Ways to communicate,

Djembe, *Bata to Banjo*

Bamboulas to banzas

Tambourines to gourds

Marimba to pan flutes

Beat to feet, *Nicolas to Savion*

Slap, Tap, to Rap

Stomp to Step, Step to Stomp

Handbone to Jazz tones

Lady Day to *Nina Simone*

Language change

Blues to Blue Notes

Codes of the past

Now we laugh to mask the pain

Funny, Funny, Funny-*Blackface*

Our DNA always finds a way

Many think it's about the *"Cool Pose"*

Now we communicate in European *"Prose"*

Verbal poets emerge and unfold

144

Cinematic Inhibition/The Window:
A Collaboration

Cinematic Inhibition

Standing on the threshold of precipitation
If I cross this line, my sense of heaven/hell/pleasure/pain
Could become one enormous distortion of compromise
The visuals are surreal, enticing, erotic, and alluring
It's a place that mama said, "Satan" lurks
It's everything a child of God is to avoid
Carnality is exploited to it highest degree.
It's Romanesque at its' microcosmic best
It's a scene that challenges the very nature of morality
But who defines morality? Man? God? God's words? Who?
Heaven is the pleasure one gets from simulated sex acts, no
penetration
Yet the body reacts
Pain is the extortion of one's financial budget
But the real pain is watching Satan in the form of *Dead
Presidents* being spent
To pleasure one's fleshy desires

I watch cautiously at flesh being used to survive one's life styles
Back rooms of moans, gropes, and grunts,
Sounds are all you hear, as fantasies are momentarily fulfilled
Egos are being catered to for the push of a Jackson, Grant, or Benjamin
She tells them what they want to hear, she tells him what he wants to hear
She tells me what I want to hear.
She whispers and echoes " big daddy, take your time, do me daddy"
"What are you working with?" $200.00 for it all. $120.00 for a blowjob.
$80.00 for a hand job. She asks, "do you have a condom?"
She becomes a cinematic inhibition at a moment's notice for a few Dead Presidents
You cum for a price! There's the touch, the lick, the squeeze, the feel, the directions, the rules of engagement. She's directing the movie. Every whim, she controls. She's preparing for her next greatest performance, cause she smells the money, she feels the money, she sees the money. There is no play, before the pay.

You stick/move/play cat/mouse/you exchange for business
sake

She

teases/pleases/seizes/appeases/pushes/pull/in/out/up/down
/over/under-moving flexible like a gymnasts, every man's
wildest fantasies being fulfilled at a moment's notices for a
dollar, a frank, a guilder, or a pound.

She claims sticky wetness, hot and horny, but it's ego
manipulation, verbal taunting

You can smell the perfume of sex in the air, and the rooms
are private

Sometimes open

Guards, non-English speaking man the protect the doors
from a distant

The rush of the thrill is addicting, it's like being hooked on
a deadly substance (crack)

You can't release this demon unless you rehab for detoxing,
Unfortunately, there is no rehab for sexaholics,

It's the zenith of economic bargaining,

It's basic economics- supply and demand, you supply the
money and she demands you cum. It's business, never
personal. She proclaims, she is not a prostitute, a madam,
or a call girl; but for the right price, when you call she'll be
at your destination at a moment's notice. She says "it's a

business and she is trying to make a living, but is tired of turning tricks. She will cum in a heartbeat to make that cash. This is fantasy, blissful surrealism. Who is she and what lurks behind those pretty brown eyes? What are her desires? Does she have goals for success in life, whatever that might be? I don't know, I never ask. Does she start her day as a waitress or student, becomes a stripper, an exotic dancer or a business woman at night? It's all for money, entertainment, and survival.

The Window

Damn, all these people, another night another dollar. I wonder who's first? Is he coming over or not? Maybe someday I can stop all this hustling. How long can I maintain this lifestyle, this dead end work? Fuck men...I have a horrible love/hate relationship with them. Sometimes I wonder what life holds for me. Men must be sick to pay for a sex service. Maybe I'm the insane one to sell my body for money. It's a living...oh well! There's nothing else I can do but this pays the bills. I don't have an education, so, I must do this to survive. But I believe in the Cinderella fairytale. One day a man will walk into this parlor and see thru me. He'll look into my eyes and see me for the woman I am. He'll rescue me from this sinful life. He'll take care of me and I'll never have to be a part of this anymore. I'll be free or will I?

Will he really see me? Will I be stuck? Dave says he loves me; but does he? I am doing him freely, but everybody else pays. I never thought I'd ever be in this situation…hey he's a cutie…Where you going sugar…uh oh who the hell is this idiot…please keep walking. Could Dave ever truly love me? He says, he does. He comes three times a week to be with me. Ugh, these tourists. Why are they always trying to snap photo? Grandpas gawking. I am so tired of it. I hear they have a play in NYC call "The Life." I think I'd love to check it out someday. A play based upon the oldest, but non-respected profession, who would have thought?

We Communicated

We communicated
From djembe to congas
drum beat to banjo
ragtime (Scot Joplin) to jazz to blue notes,
Without drum beat, we used our feet
From Tap To Stomp
From Lindy Hop To Break Dance
Bogoloo Robot, Strut,
We tapped, stepped,
We communicated

Skin I'm In

Guest Worker System-1940
Farmer owners & Factory owners apply
Special visas are granted?
Workers flood this country.

The law is a pretty good one.
Who checks the conditions of these workers?
They work under brutally controlled conditions.
Sometimes they are locked up.

European girls, young-teenaged, nice, middle-class
Who comes over, desiring to be an *au pair*!
They're granted a special visa-The *J1*.
The amenities: guarantees, inspections, monitoring
Orientation classes, education provisions. Fantastic!
A wonderful cultural experience is bestowed,   and
A chance for better education, aspires.

West African girls, young-teenaged, nice rural-class
Who comes over, desiring to be an *au pair*!
They're granted a special-special visa- *B1*.
The amenities: no guarantees, no monitors, no orientations.

151

No classes, no education provisions, no inspections.
A different cultural experience under siege
Development is arrested and...
Passports are checked at the airport!

The *Maafa* continues...
Sounds like a conduit into enslavement.
Another young domestic worker, lost!
Is this *Slavery By Another Name*?

Track the B1 visas; find *Traces of the Trade*
The content of skin lies not.
Skin is *vilified* and *institutionalized.*

6 Arr. Rue Monsieur Le Prince

History has a way of finding you
The plaque on the wall inscribed:
L'homme de lettres noir Americain
Richard Wright habitat cet immeuble de 1948 a 1959
Right above this book store lived America's *Black Boy*
Native Son

Not so far away is San Francisco Book Company (American
owned)
It sells and buys used books. Bay Area feet often trod *Rue
Monsieur Le Prince*
I was introduced to the owner. A friendly fellow, I thought.

He said, "I have come across your book *Black Man in
Europe.*"
Who would have guessed it, *Un Homme de Race Noire en
Europe, my book*
In an American book store in France, on the same block
where Richard
Wright lived for 11 years.

6 Arrt. Place Saint-Germain Des Pres

wealth infiltrates every sinew & marrow of this ancient-
modern *Arridismont*
a heartbeat of gaudiness envelops the residence fabric
expensive
boutiques & shops   isolating
themselves because the money   induces *this* permission

poor folk intersects with the riche, begging or performing

an outsider, I am, naïve & privy to this level of privileged
wealth

Stand
co-mingling,
code-switching,
watching
smiling
and   spending money

being an *illusion* indulging dream-world possibilities

154

who what have thought a native black boy from the *7th Ward*
Saint Anthony Street   New Orleans

would be walking the streets of the *Saint Germain's*
district   of   Paris?

whoever said black dreams were real?

Alvin Ailey in Berkeley & Paris

I enjoyed 20 years of Ailey at Zellerbach (2009)
50 years of entertainment   elegance
dance artistry personified   satisfying
and Judith Jamison is still holding court
timeless as a choreographed *Revelations*

My eight year old niece loved the show.

I still recall her saying, "Uncle, I thought Alvin Ailey
was an all Black dance production; why are there white
people
on stage dancing?"

I replied, "*yes it is, but let's discuss it later, enjoy the show.*"

Shhh…be quiet and watch!

Paris three months later…
Sauntering Ville de Neuilly sur Seine on Avenue du
Chateau
I enter station de metro Pont de Neuilly

156

posters emboss impressions on Metro walls:
Les etes de la danse de paris
Theatre du Chatelet du 6 au 25 Juillet 2009
Alvin Ailey-American Dance Theater

Four sculpted Black men loom in speedos bare-chested
suspended in air…
on display

Negro Identity

A Southern baby boy born into a Negro identity circa 1969
Walked into Black identity during the 1970s

Another beginning, another decade another *identity*
The Black experience is always
transitioning
transforming &
redefining
Ran into the 1980s as an Afro-American
Lived Reaganomics and identity selection & got a
consensus on the Census

Stood proud as an African-American in the 1990s
Couldn't be more proud of my selection of self-identity

Cruised into the 21st Century & two decades later
I am confounded, confused, conflicted, and disturbed at
our so-called post-racial status; but if post-racial, why the
problems?

News flash: Is Race Still an Issue In America?

158

A bi-racial baby is denied burial in a small town in Georgia 1996

Oscar Grant executed on the Fruitvale Bart Station platform on New Year's morning 2009

Six high school students convicted of egregious crimes in Jena, Louisiana 2006

A white judge refuses to marry a black & white couple-Louisiana 2009

Young people are afraid to pursue their college education in state schools in California due to racially charged environments – nooses hanging in libraries??? 2010
People attend town hall meetings by the 44th President of the United States strapped with assault rifles – and they're not law enforcement…would this have happened with the Bush Administration? 2009

"I forgot he was Black for an hour." –Chris Matthews

All black people are ordered to leave a Wal-Mart in southern New Jersey over the public address system. 2010

It's an all out assault on Black people…the calendar has been reversed and we tap dance and bridle our tongues…

I am politically categorized as a person of African descent, and I don't feel American because of contention
It seems like I have changed self-description more than a leopard changes his spots

In 2010 the Census reads: Black, African-American, or Negro [check the box]

I thought our parents killed Jim Crow? Maybe crow is hard to kill while in stealth mode?

Will I be seen as a hyphenation, American, Black, or Negro? You make the call…

9. **What is Person 1's race?** Mark X one or more boxes.
☐ White
☐ Black, African Am., or Negro
☐ American Indian or Alaska Native — Print name of enrolled or principal tribe. ↗

Nathan Jones is a poet, a storyteller, and the author of Revolutionary Erotica, Black Man In Europe: The Novel, Black Man In Europe: Micro-Volume I, and Excerpts From My Soul...Read Without Prejudice. He is an educator who takes pleasure in working with urban youth in his community. He currently resides in Oakland, California.

Other Books by Nathan Jones

Revolutionary Erotica

Black Man In Europe: The Novel

Black Man In Europe: Micro-Volume I

Forthcoming Projects from Nathan Jones

Letters To My Daughter: How A Dad Became A
Father

In The Moment: A Collection of Poetry

The Paris Chronicles

Love's Reflection

Letters: Voices From The Past

Connect with Me Online

www.sajetanira.com